[S.S. 534.]

NOTE.—This Pamphlet cancels :—
S.S. 419, Supplement to S.S. 419, S.S. 419a, S.S. 419b, S.S. 111, S.S. 111a, S.S. 111b, S.S. 111c, S.S. 125, S.S. 127, S.S. 128, S.S. 129, and S.S. 453.

DEFENSIVE MEASURES

AGAINST

GAS ATTACKS.

Every Officer is responsible that the men under his command are properly instructed in Defensive Measures against Gas Attacks, that all appliances are at all times in perfect order and that Standing Orders on the subject are thoroughly understood. During a Gas Attack it is important that all measures taken should be carried out with the utmost calm in order to avoid confusion and waste of energy.

The Naval & Military Press Ltd

Published by

The Naval & Military Press Ltd
Unit 5 Riverside, Brambleside
Bellbrook Industrial Estate
Uckfield, East Sussex
TN22 1QQ England

Tel: +44 (0)1825 749494

www.naval-military-press.com
www.nmarchive.com

*In reprinting in facsimile from the original, any imperfections are inevitably reproduced
and the quality may fall short of modern type and cartographic standards.*

Defensive Measures Against Gas Attacks.

I.—INTRODUCTION.

A.—GENERAL CONSIDERATIONS.

1. The following notes on defensive measures against hostile gas attacks have been compiled for the guidance of regimental officers in instructing their men and giving orders on this subject. They deal chiefly with the preparations necessary to combat such attacks successfully, and with the action to be taken during and subsequent to an attack.

2. In the absence of suitable means of protection the poison gases used in war are extremely deadly and the breathing of only very small quantities of them may cause death or serious injury. This being the case, it is essential that not the slightest time should be lost in putting on the box respirator or helmet on the gas alarm being given.

It cannot be too strongly insisted on that the measures which have been elaborated to meet hostile gas attacks afford **perfect protection,** and if they are carried out properly no one will suffer from gas poisoning.

3. The whole basis of protecting troops against gas lies (*a*) in keeping the appliances in perfect working order; (*b*) in learning to adjust them rapidly under all conditions; and (*c*) in ensuring that every man is given immediate warning. These results can only be attained:

(i) **By frequent and thorough inspection of all protective appliances.**

(ii) **By thorough instruction and training in their use.**

(iii) **By every man understanding and complying with all Standing Orders on the subject of defence against gas.**

If these are effectually carried out, there is nothing to fear from hostile gas attacks. Officers must impress this on their men, as an important object of all anti-gas instruction should be to inspire complete confidence in the efficacy of **the** methods which are adopted.

B.—NATURE OF GAS ATTACKS.

(i) GAS CLOUDS.

4. This method of making a gas attack is entirely dependent on the direction of the wind. The gas is carried up to the trenches compressed in steel cylinders. These are dug in at the bottom of the trench and connected with pipes leading out over the parapet. When the valves of the cylinders are opened, the gas escapes with a hissing sound, which, on a still night, can frequently be heard at a considerable distance. It mixes with the air and is carried by the wind towards the opposing trenches, spreading out as it goes forward. A continuous wave of gas and air is thus formed, the colour of which may vary

    (*a*) Because of the weather conditions. In very dry air it may be almost transparent and slightly greenish in colour while in damp weather it forms a white cloud.

    (*b*) Because it may be mixed with smoke of any colour.

5. A cloud attack can only take place when there is a steady but not too strong wind blowing from the enemy's lines towards our own. A wind between 4 and 8 miles an hour is the most likely condition. An 8-mile wind will carry the gas cloud twice as quickly as a man walks rapidly.

Gas attacks may occur at any time of the day, but are most likely to be made during the night or in the early morning.

Gentle rain is without appreciable effect on a gas attack, but strong rain washes down the gas. Fogs have hardly any effect, and may, in fact, be taken advantage of to make an attack unexpectedly. Watercourses and ponds are no obstruction to a gas cloud.

6. The gas used by the enemy is generally a mixture of chlorine and phosgene, both of which are strongly asphyxiating. The gases are heavier than air, and therefore tend to flow along the ground and into trenches, shelters, craters and hollows. The gas cloud may flow round slight eminences, thus leaving patches of country which remain free from gas.

7. Chlorine and phosgene strongly attack the mucous membranes of the respiratory organs, causing bad coughing. In strong concentrations of gas, or by longer exposure to low concentrations, the lungs are injured and breathing becomes more and more difficult and and eventually impossible, so that the unprotected man dies of suffocation. Death is sometimes caused by two or three breaths of the gas. Even when very dilute, chlorine can be recognised by its peculiar smell, which is like chloride of lime, but stronger and more irritating.

Both chlorine and phosgene also exert a strongly corrosive action on metals, so that the metal parts of arms must be carefully protected by greasing them.

8. The speed with which the gas cloud approaches depends entirely on the wind velocity. Gas attacks have been made with wind velocities varying from 3 to 20 miles per hour, *i.e.*, from 1½ to 10 yards per second. In a 9-mile wind, the gas would reach trenches 100 yards distant in 20 seconds.

Gas attacks have been made on fronts varying from 1 to 5 miles; their effects at points up to 8 miles behind the front trenches have been sufficiently severe to make it necessary to wear helmets.

(ii) GAS PROJECTILES.

9. The use of these is not entirely dependent on the direction of the wind. In gas projectiles such as shells, hand grenades, and trench mortar bombs, a part or the whole of the explosive charge is replaced by a liquid which is converted into gas by the explosion. The explosive force and noise of detonation of these projectiles is less than that of the ordinary kind, and a large number of them are usually discharged into a comparatively small space. After the explosion, the irritant chemicals form a small gas cloud, though some may sink to the ground and remain active for a considerable time.

For using gas shells, the best condition is calm, or with a wind of low velocity.

Gas projectiles can be used in all types of country. Woods, bushes and cornfields and clumps of buildings may hold the gas active for a considerable time.

10. Two kinds of shell gases are used by the enemy, viz., **lachrymators,** which mainly affect the eyes, and **poison gases,** which may affect the eyes and are just as deadly as the gases used in the form of clouds.

(i) TEAR, OR LACHRYMATORY SHELLS.

These shells on explosion drive the liquid chemical which they contain into the air as a mist. They cause the eyes to water strongly and thereby gradually put men out of action.

Their actual smell may be slight. Large concentrations of lachrymators begin to affect the lungs and cause sickness, coughing and general irritation.

(ii) POISON SHELLS.

Besides the comparatively harmless lachrymators the enemy also uses projectiles which contain a gas, the action of which is very similar to that of phosgene. Because of their slight detonation, these shells are liable to be mistaken for blinds, but they emit large quantities of a gas which attacks the lungs strongly, and is very dangerous, and even in slight cases may cause serious after-effects.

(iii) SMOKE.

11. The enemy may make use of smoke, either in the form of a cloud or emitted from shells and bombs. Smoke may be used with gas or between gas clouds; it may also be used alone to distract attention from a real discharge of gas, to cover the advance of infantry, or merely as a false gas attack.

(iv) MINE AND EXPLOSION GASES.

12. The poisonous gases which occur in mines, and which are formed in large quantities when high explosive goes off in an enclosed space, e.g., from a direct hit in a shelter, or on the explosion of a charge in a mine, are not protected against by the ordinary anti-gas appliances. The chief of these gases is carbon monoxide. Protection against such gases will not be considered in these notes. It is fully dealt with in C.D.S. 308 (Memorandum on Gas Poisoning in Mines).

II.—ORGANISATION OF GAS DEFENCE.

13. **Officers are held responsible that all the anti-gas appliances for protecting their men are maintained in perfect condition, and that all ranks under their command are thoroughly trained in the use of these appliances and in all other measures which may affect their safety against gas.**

14. **Summary of Protective Measures.**

  (a) Provision to each man of individual protective devices.

  (b) Arrangement for the inspection of those appliances and training in their use and instruction in all other measures of gas defence.

  (c) Provision of protected and gas-proof shelters.

  (d) Weather observations to determine periods when the conditions are favourable to a hostile gas attack.

  (e) Arrangement of signals and messages for immediate warning of a gas attack.

  (f) Provision of appliances for clearing gas from trenches and shelters.

A.—ORGANISATION OF ANTI-GAS DUTIES.

15. All ranks must be fully conversant with the measures to be adopted for defence against gas attacks as laid down in the Standing Orders of their formation or unit.*

---

* For typical Divisional Standing Orders, see Appendix IV.

A special **Gas Officer** is appointed in each Division, so that technical advice is readily available on all matters connected with gas defence. This officer is also charged with all duties at the Divisional Anti-Gas School. Apart from this, the following scheme of anti-gas duties should be adopted within units.

A.—ANTI-GAS DUTIES WITHIN AN INFANTRY BATTALION.

(To be modified for other units to suit their organisation and duties.)

16. The Commanding Officer will be directly responsible for all measures against gas attacks, and Company Commanders will be responsible to the C.O. for all anti-gas measures within their companies.

In each Company one N.C.O., who has been trained at an Anti-Gas School, and who has been recommended by the Divisional Gas Officer as suitable for duty as " Company Gas N.C.O.," will be specially detailed to assist the Company Commander in anti-gas measures. At least one other similarly trained and recommended N.C.O. will be immediately available to take the place of the Gas N.C.O. in case of need.

A similarly trained Gas N.C.O. will be detailed to Battalion H.Q. for duty with H.Q. details.

17. The special duties of Gas N.C.Os. will be definitely laid down in Battalions.* Other duties may, however, be performed, provided that these do not interfere with the gas duties laid down.

18. In order to secure the necessary training in all matters pertaining to defence against gas attacks, the following officers and N.C.O.'s should attend a course at the Divisional Anti-Gas School

(a) **Officers.**
   (i) The Commanding Officer or Second in Command, and the Medical Officer.
   (ii) All Company Commanders.
   (iii) Other Officers and Warrant Officers, if and when possible.

(b) **N.C.Os.**
   (i) Two per Company and per Battalion H.Q.
   (ii) Supplementary N.C.Os. to be trained whenever possible, so as to have a reserve from which to draw to replace Gas N.C.Os. in case of need.

---
* For typical Standing Orders for Company Gas N.C.Os., see Appendix V.

The selected N.C.Os. who attend the Divisional Anti-Gas Schools will be reported on by the Divisional Gas Officer as follows :—At the end of the course the Divisional Gas Officer will, if the N.C.O. is, in his opinion, suitable for duty as " Company Gas N.C.O." notify the C.O. concerned to this effect. The latter will then cause the words " Passed Anti-Gas School " to be entered in his pay book. Only N.C.Os. who have been thus reported on favourably will be detailed for duty as Company Gas N.C.Os.

19. C.Os. will facilitate in every way the duties of the Divisional Gas Officer and his N.C.Os. in visiting their lines and inspecting anti-gas arrangements, testing Strombos horn cylinders, &c., They should take every opportunity of consulting with the Divisional Gas Officer on all technical questions relating to anti-gas measures within their lines.

B.—PERSONAL ANTI-GAS EQUIPMENT.
(i) EQUIPMENT CARRIED.

20. Each man is provided with a small box respirator, a P.H. helmet and a pair of goggles. He must be made to realise that these appliances are **personal equipment, that they are of importance second only to his weapons, and that his life may depend on looking after them and keeping them in good order.**

21. The small box respirator is the most important protective apparatus. It is always to be used first in case of a gas attack, unless special orders are issued to the contrary. It will protect against all poisonous gases with the exception of mine and explosion gases, and will not become exhausted for hours, even in concentrations of gas normally unobtainable in the field.

22. The P.H. helmet is an emergency or reserve defence. It is only to be used if the owner should not have a box respirator or if the latter should be found, for any reason, to be defective. The helmet protects against all poisonous gases used by the enemy, but it does not give complete protection against heavy bombardment by lachrymatory shells.

It is not possible to put the P.H. helmet on as quickly as the small box respirator.

23. The rubber-sponge goggles are intended for use in areas which have been subjected to a bombardment with lachrymatory shells, and in which the concentration of the lachrymator is so reduced that the air can be breathed without discomfort, though effect on the eyes remains. It must be remembered that after such a bombardment, the tear-producing effect may persist, even in the open, for several hours, and in trenches, dug-outs, cellars, &c., it **may last for over a day.**

(ii) WHEN AND WHERE CARRIED.

24. (*a*) All three appliances should be carried within three miles of the front line.

(*b*) When the wind is safe, working parties during work and at the discretion of the officer in command may take off their box respirators, provided the latter are placed conveniently at hand for use in case of a sudden gas shell attack or change of wind. The P.H. helmet will always be carried.

(*c*) At distances greater than three miles the P.H. helmet and goggles only need be carried, the box respirators being kept with the equipment under arrangements by the O.C. of the Unit.

C.—PROTECTION OF SHELTERS.
(i) METHODS OF PROTECTION.

25. Protection of dug-outs, cellars, buildings, &c., is given if all entrances are closed by well-fitting doors or by blankets sprayed with hypo. solution from a Vermorel sprayer. Practically no gas passes through a wet blanket, and the protection depends on getting a good joint at the sides and bottom of a doorway, so as to stop all draughts. This can be effected by letting the blanket rest on battens, fixed with a slight slope, against the door frame. The blanket should overlap the outer sides and a fold should lie on the ground at the bottom. A pole is fastened to the blanket, which allows the latter to be rolled up on the frame and causes it to fall evenly.

26. Wherever possible, particularly where there is likely to be movement in and out of the shelter, two blankets fitted in this way but sloping in opposite directions should be provided. There should be an interval of at least 3 feet between the two frames, and the larger this vestibule is made, the more efficient is the dug-out.

When not in use, the blankets should be rolled up and held so that they can be readily released, and should be sprayed occasionaly with water or a little Vermorel sprayer solution.

If the blankets become stiff from a deposit of chemicals, they should be sprayed with water.

27. All ranks must be taught how to use gas-proof dug-outs, *e.g.*, how to enter a protected doorway quickly, replacing the blanket immediately, and carrying in as little outside air as possible.

28. The protection afforded by these means is just as complete against lachrymatory gases as it is against cloud gas and poisonous shell gases.

(ii) SHELTERS WHICH SHOULD BE PROTECTED.

29. The following should always be protected:—
    Medical aid-posts and advanced dressing stations, Company, Battalion and Brigade Headquarters, Signal Shelters and any other place where work has to be carried out during a gas attack.

30. In addition to the above, it is desirable to protect all dugouts, cellars and buildings within the shell area, particularly those of artillery personnel. It should be noted, however, that the protection of dug-outs for troops in the front line of trenches is usually inadvisable on account of the delay involved in getting men out in time of attack. It is desirable to protect stretcher bearers' dug-outs with a view to putting casualties in them.

D.—PROTECTION OF WEAPONS AND EQUIPMENT.

31. Arms and ammunition and the metal parts of special equipment (*e.g.*, telephone instruments) must be carefully protected against gas by greasing them or keeping them completely covered. Otherwise, particularly in damp weather, they may rust or corrode so badly as to refuse to act. A mineral oil must be used for this purpose. The following in particular should be protected :—

(i) SMALL ARMS AND S.A.A.

32. Machine guns and rifles must be kept carefully cleaned and well oiled. The effects of corrosion of ammunition are of even more importance than the direct effects of gas upon machine guns and rifles.

Ammunition boxes must be kept closed. Vickers belts should be kept in their boxes until actually required for use. The wooden belt boxes are fairly gas-tight, but the metal belt boxes should be made gas-tight by inserting strips of flannelette in the joint between the lid and the box.

Lewis magazines should be kept in some form of box, the joints of which are made as gas-tight as possible with flannelette.

A recess should be made, high up in the parapet if possible, for storing ammunition and guns. A blanket curtain, moistened with water or Vermorel sprayer solution, will greatly assist in keeping the gas out.

(ii) HAND AND RIFLE GRENADES.

33. Unboxed grenades should be kept covered as far as possible. All safety pins and working parts, especially those made of brass, should be kept oiled to prevent their setting from corrosion by the gas. In the case of No. 20 and No. 24 Rifle Grenades, oil should be worked in as much as possible under the sleeve retaining the studs, as these are liable to become set. The rods also require the same treatment.

(iii) LIGHT TRENCH MORTARS AND THEIR AMMUNITION.

34. As far as the supply of oil permits, the bore and all bright parts of light trench mortars and their spare parts should be kept permanently oiled. When not in use, mortars should be covered with sacking or similar material.

Unboxed ammunition should be kept covered as far as possible and the bright parts oiled immediately after arrival. Ammunition which has been in store for some time should be used up first.

(iv) GUNS, MEDIUM AND HEAVY TRENCH MORTARS AND THEIR AMMUNITION.

35. The protection of artillery and artillery ammunition is dealt with in para. 116.

(v) SIGNALS EQUIPMENT.

36. The protection of signals equipment is dealt with in para. 123.

E.—WIND OBSERVATION.

37. The Meteorological Service, R.E., reports to Headquarters of Formations whenever the wind passes into a dangerous quarter, showing the direction and strength of the wind. As a result of these reports, " Gas Alert " is ordered by Corps or Divisional H.Q. These general reports, however, refer to large tracts of country and it is possible that on isolated lengths of front, conditions of terrain or the alignment of the trenches may permit of local air currents which are favourable to the enemy. It is essential, therefore, that the troops themselves should be on the look-out for the possibility of a gas attack. For this purpose Company Commanders are responsible that wind observations are made on their Company front every three hours, or oftener if the wind is in, or approaching, a dangerous quarter, and the reports forwarded through the usual channels to Brigade H.Q. For the method of making these observations and preparing the reports, see Appendix VI.

F.—THE GAS ALERT PERIOD.

(i) ORDER FOR GAS ALERT.

38. Gas Alert will be ordered when the wind is in the dangerous quarter, no matter what the strength of the wind.

The order " Gas Alert " will be sent out to all units by Corps H.Q. (or, if authority has been so delegated, by Divisional H.Q.), but Brigade H.Q. or Battalion Commanders are empowered to order a " Gas Alert " as a result of wind observations forwarded by Company Commanders. Such action will be reported immediately to the next higher formation.

Gas Alert notices should be posted at the entrance to each main communication trench and at other suitable points within Divisional Areas.

(ii) PRECAUTIONS DURING GAS ALERT.

(a) Inspection.

39. All box respirators and helmets should be carefully inspected and the inspection should be repeated daily. Steps must be taken to ascertain that all gas alarm appliances are in their position and in good order.

(b) Alert position of respirators and helmets.

40. All ranks within one mile of the front line must carry their box respirators (or their helmets, should they have no box respirators) in the alert position. The press buttons of the flap of the box respirator satchel must be unfastened.

During Gas Alert the chin strap of the steel helmet must on no account be worn under the chin, as it will impede the rapid adjustment of the respirator or helmet.

(c) Special Orders for men using the P.H. Helmet.

41. The two upper buttons of both jacket and greatcoat will be left undone. Men are forbidden to wear mackintosh sheets round their necks.

In no circumstances will anything (rifle, field glasses, &c.) be slung across the chest in such a manner as to interfere with the rapid adjustment of the helmet.

Jackets will not be taken off within one mile of the front line.

(d) Sentries, &c.

42. A sentry should be posted at each Strombos horn or other alarm device and instructed in its use and all working parties should have a sentry posted to give instant warning of a gas attack.

A sentry should be posted to every large shelter or group of small shelters and also to each Headquarters, Signal Office and each independent body of men.

Arrangements must be made by the officer in charge of the trench for warning the Artillery Observation Post if there is one in the trench.

Commanders of units in billets within 8 miles of the front line trenches must organise a system of giving the alarm and rousing all men in cellars or houses.

At night sentries should have at least two men within reach of them, so that the alarm can be spread rapidly.

(e) Sleeping.

43. When a gas attack is probable, men in front line trenches should sleep on the fire step instead of in dug-outs. Men sleeping

in rearward lines, or in works where they are allowed to take off their equipment, must sleep with their box respirators on the person.

(f) **Company Gas N.C.Os.**

44. Company Gas N.C.Os. will report to Company H.Q. in readiness to assist the Company Commander should a gas attack occur.

45. **Officers and N.C.Os. in command of any unit or party must see that the above orders are strictly carried out, both for troops in front line trenches and for detached bodies of troops (working and carrying parties, &c.).**

(g) **Ammonia Capsules.**

46. Medical Officers must see that a proper proportion of the ammonia capsules are with stretcher bearers in the front line, in readiness for their immediate use after a gas attack.

(iii) REMOVAL OF GAS ALERT.

47. Gas Alert will not be taken off without the authority of the Corps Commander or the Divisional Commander to whom authority has been delegated.

On the receipt of orders for the removal of Gas Alert, the notices on the subject will be amended accordingly.

G.—GAS ALARM.

(i) METHOD OF GIVING THE ALARM.

48. For the purpose of giving the alarm the Strombos horn, which is audible for very long distances, is the most important appliance. Its main use is for conveying the alarm to troops in support and reserve lines. In addition some local appliance, such as a gong or suspended rail, must be fitted up at every sentry's post for the purpose of rousing the men in the immediate vicinity and for conveying the alarm to the sentries in charge of the Strombos horns.

Strombos horns should be in the front line, at intervals ordinarily not greater than 400 yards, and at such other points behind the front as required to ensure transmission of warning. As much use as possible should be made of the telephone for transmitting the gas alarm, though it cannot be relied upon owing to the possibility of its breaking down.

No reliance can be placed on methods of giving the alarm involving the use of the lungs, *e.g.*, bugles or whistles.

49. Sentries must be prepared to give the alarm on the first appearance of gas, as a few seconds delay may involve very serious consequences. Signals must be passed along by all sentries as soon as heard.

The earliest warning of a gas attack is given :—

(a) By the noise of the gas escaping from the cylinders.

(b) By the appearance of a cloud of any colour over the enemy's trenches. If the attack takes place at night, the cloud will not be visible from a distance.

(c) By the smell of the gas in listening posts.

(ii) ACTION TO BE TAKEN IN THE TRENCHES ON GAS ALARM.

50. (a) **Respirators** to be put on immediately by all ranks (a helmet, if no box respirator is available).

(b) **Rouse** all men in trenches, dug-outs and mine shafts, warn officers and artillery observation posts and all employed men.

(c) **Artillery Support** to be called for by Company Commanders, by means of prearranged signals.

(d) **Warn** Battalion H.Q. and troops in rear.

(e) **All ranks stand to arms** in the front trenches and elsewhere where the tactical situation demands.

(f) **Blanket curtains** at entrances to protected shelters to be let down and carefully fixed.

(g) **Movement** to cease except where necessary.

(iii) ACTION TO BE TAKEN IN BILLETS AND BACK AREAS.

51. (a) All men in cellars or houses to be roused.

(b) The blanket curtains of protected cellars, &c., to be let down and fixed in position.

(c) Box respirators to be put on immediately the gas is apparent.

H.—ACTION DURING A GAS ATTACK.

(i) PROTECTIVE MEASURES.

52 There should be as little moving about and talking as possible in the trenches. Men must be made to realise that with the gas now used by the enemy, observance of this may be essential for their safety.

When an attack is in progress, all bodies of troops or transport on the move should halt and all working parties cease work until the gas cloud has passed.

If a relief is going on, units should stand fast as far as possible until the gas cloud has passed.

Supports and parties bringing up bombs should only be moved up if the tactical situation demands it.

53. If troops in support or reserve lines of trenches remain in, or go into, dug-outs, they must continue to wear their anti-gas appliances.

Officers and N.C.Os. must on no account remove or open up the masks of the box respirators or raise their helmets to give orders. The breathing tube may be removed from the mouth when it is necessary to speak, but it must be replaced.

54. Men must always be on the look-out to help each other in case a box respirator or helmet is damaged by fire or accident. When a man is wounded, he must be watched to see that he does not remove his respirator or helmet until he is safely inside a protected shelter; if necessary, his hands should be tied.

Men must be warned that if they are slightly gassed before adjusting their respirators or helmets they must not remove them. The effect will wear off.

(ii) **TACTICAL MEASURES.**

55. From the point of view of protection against gas, nothing is gained by men remaining in unprotected dug-outs or by moving to a flank or to the rear. It is, therefore, desirable that on tactical and disciplinary grounds all men in the front line of trenches should be forbidden to do these things. In support or reserve lines, where there are protected dug-outs, it is advisable for men to stay in them unless the tactical situation makes it desirable for them to come out.

56. Nothing is gained by opening rapid rifle fire unless the enemy's infantry attacks. A slow rate of fire from rifles and occasional short bursts of fire from machine guns will lessen the chance of their jamming from the action of the gas and tends to occupy and steady the infantry.

57. It should be remembered that the enemy's infantry cannot attack while the gas discharge is in progress and is unlikely to do so for an appreciable time—at least 10 minutes—after it has ceased. It is, in fact, a common practice for the enemy infantry to retire to the second and third line of trench whilst gas is being discharged. There is, therefore, no object in opening an intense S.O.S. barrage of artillery on "No man's land" during the actual gas cloud and it is advisable that the warning to the Artillery of a gas attack should be a signal differing from the ordinary S.O.S. signal, as the latter may have to be sent later if an infantry attack develops.

58. It must be remembered that smoke may be used by the enemy at the same time as, or alternately with, the gas and that under cover of a smoke cloud he may send out assaulting or raiding parties. A careful look-out must, therefore, be kept; hostile patrols or raiders may be frustrated by cross-fire of rifles and machine guns and should an assault develop the ordinary S.O.S. procedure should be carried out.

I.—PRECAUTIONS AGAINST GAS SHELLS.

59. Owing to the small explosion which occurs with these shells, they are liable to be mistaken for blinds, and even when the gas is smelt men may not realise its possibly dangerous character at once and so may delay putting on respirators or helmets until too late. Men sleeping in dug-outs may be seriously affected unless they are roused. Men in the open air are unlikely to be seriously affected by poison gas shells, provided they put on respirators or helmets on first experiencing the gas. The following points should therefore be attended to :—

60. (i) All shells which explode with a small detonation or appear to be blind should be regarded with particular attention ; the respirator or helmet should be put on at the first indication of gas and blanket protection of shelters adjusted.

(ii) Arrangements must be made for giving a LOCAL alarm in the event of a sudden and intense bombardment with poison gas shells, but care must be taken that this alarm is not confused with the main alarm. Strombos horns must on no account be used to give warning of a gas shell bombardment.

(iii) All shelters in the vicinity of an area bombarded with poison gas shells must be visited and any sleeping men roused.

(iv) Box respirators or helmets should continue to be worn throughout the area bombarded with poison gas shells until the order is given by the local unit Commander for their removal.

61. Lachrymatory or "tear" shells are frequently used by the enemy for the purpose of hindering the movements of troops, for preventing the bringing up of supports, or for interfering with the action of artillery.

Owing to the deadly nature of poison gas shells, however, **the precautions given in para. 60 above must be taken for all gas shells.** The goggles are intended for use after *lachrymatory* bombardments only, in cases where the irritant gas persists in the neighbourhood of shell holes, &c.

J.—PRECAUTIONS TO BE TAKEN WITH REGARD TO OUR OWN USE OF GAS IN CYLINDERS, BOMBS, &c.

62. Protection of troops is necessary during our own gas attacks. Adequate protective measures should always be possible, as arrangements can be made in advance and the element of surprise can be excluded. The following points should be noted :—

(i) HANDLING GAS CYLINDERS.

63. Men engaged in carrying or digging-in gas cylinders should carry their box respirators in the "Alert" position.

(ii) ACTION WHEN GAS CYLINDERS ARE IN POSITION IN TRENCHES.

64. (a) Box respirators should be carried in the "Alert" position by troops in front line trenches.

(b) If a cylinder is burst by shell-fire, men should retire up-wind for a short distance, if possible. Dug-outs in the neighbourhood of the burst must be evacuated at once.

(iii) ACTION DURING OUR GAS ATTACKS.

65. (a) It is advisable that all troops, except those whose presence is considered absolutely necessary, should be withdrawn from the front trench before gas is discharged. Any officer or man who has special orders to remain must *wear* his box respirator.

(b) All troops in any part of the line within half a mile of the nearest point where gas is being discharged must *wear* their box respirators.

(c) If troops advance after a cloud gas attack has been made, it must be remembered that the gas may hang about for a considerable time in long grass, shell holes and hollows, and for several hours in the enemy's shelters. Raiding or reconnoitring parties after a gas discharge should carry their respirators in the Alert position. Dug-outs should not be occupied until they have been thoroughly ventilated and the absence of gas established. This is equally necessary with regard to shelters which have been penetrated by gas from shells or bombs.

(iv) GAS BOMBS AND GRENADES.

66. These may, if necessary, be stored with other ammunition. In the event of leakage they should be buried in the ground $3\frac{1}{2}$ feet deep. They should not be thrown into water. All rescue work and disposal of leaky shells should be carried out by men wearing box respirators.

K.—ACTION SUBSEQUENT TO A GAS ATTACK.

(i) GENERAL.

67. **The most important measure to be taken after a cloud gas attack is to prepare for a further attack.** The enemy frequently sends several successive waves of gas at intervals varying from a few minutes up to several hours and it is therefore necessary to be on the alert to combat this procedure. The following measures should be adopted as soon as the gas cloud has passed :—

(a) **Removal of respirators.**—Anti-gas fans should be used to assist in clearing the trenches of gas, so as to admit of respirators being removed. Box respirators and helmets must not be removed until permission has been given by the Company Commander, who will, when possible, ascertain from officers and N.C.O's. who have been trained at a Divisional Gas School that it is safe to do so.

(b) **Return to the Alert position.**—So as to be ready for a subsequent attack, box respirators and helmets must be put back in the Alert position.

A sharp look-out must be kept for a repetition of the gas attack, as long as the wind continues in a dangerous quarter.

(ii) MOVEMENT.

68. Owing to the enemy gas sometimes causing bad after-effects, which are intensified by subsequent exertion, the following points should be attended to:—

(a) No man suffering from the effects of gas, however slightly, should be allowed to walk to the dressing station.

(b) The clearing of the trenches and dug-outs should not be carried out by men who have been affected by the gas.

(c) After a gas attack, troops in the front trenches should be relieved of all fatigue and carrying work for 24 hours by sending up working parties from companies in rear.

(d) Horses which have been exposed to the gas should not be worked for 24 hours if it can be avoided.

(iii) CLEARING DUG-OUTS AND OTHER SHELTERS.

69. It is essential that no dug-out be entered after a gas attack, except with box respirators or helmets adjusted, until it has been ascertained that it is free from gas. The only efficient method of clearing dug-outs from gas is by thorough ventilation. The older method of spraying is not efficient.

An appreciable quantity of gas may be retained in the clothing of men exposed to gas attacks and also in bedding, coats, &c., left in shelters. Precautions should, therefore, be taken to air all clothing.

(a) **Ventilation.**

70. **Natural Ventilation.**—Unless a shelter has been thoroughly ventilated by artificial means, as described below, it must not be slept in, or occupied without wearing respirators, until at least 12 hours have elapsed. It must not be entered at all without respirators on for at least 3 hours. The above refers to cloud gas attacks. In

the case of gas shell bombardments the times cannot be definitely stated, as they depend on the nature of the gas used and the severity of the bombardment. With lachrymatory gases the times after which shelters can be used without discomfort may be considerably longer than those mentioned above.

71. **Ventilation by Fire.**—All kinds of shelters can be efficiently and rapidly cleared of gas by the use of fires. Shelters with two openings are the easiest to ventilate and where possible dug-outs with only one entrance should have a second opening made, even a very small one, to assist in ventilation.

In dug-outs provided with a single exit at the end of a short passage the best results are obtained if the fire is placed in the centre of the floor of the dug-out and at a height of about 6 inches.

In dug-outs provided with a single exit at the end of a long and nearly horizontal passage the best results are obtained if the fire is placed about one-third of the distance from the inner end of the passage.

In dug-outs provided with two or more exits the fire should be placed at the inner end of one of the exit passages.

72. In general, 1 lb. of dry wood per 200 cubic feet of air space is sufficient for clearance of any gas. The best fuel is split wood, but any fuel which does not smoulder or give off thick smoke can be used. The materials for the fire, e.g., the split wood, newspaper, and a small bottle of paraffin for lighting purposes, should be kept in a sandbag enclosed in a biscuit tin provided with a lid. An improvised brazier should be kept ready for use.

The fire must be kept burning for at least ten minutes and the atmosphere in the shelter should be tested from time to time.

73. **Ventilation by Fanning.**—Dug-outs can be ventilated by producing air currents in them by means of special anti-gas fans. A full description of the anti-gas fan and the method of using it to clear gas from trenches and shelters is given later (see paras. 102-106).

If no anti-gas fans are available, ventilation can be assisted by flapping with improvised fans such as sandbags, ground sheets, &c.

(b) **Sprayers.**

74. The use of Vermorel sprayers for clearing gas from trenches and shelters has been given up. The hypo. solution has very little effect on phosgene and even with the addition of other chemicals it cannot be relied upon to remove this gas from the air. Vermorel sprayers have consequently been withdrawn from general use.

(iv) CLEANING OF ARMS AND AMMUNITION.

75. Rifles and machine guns must be cleaned after a gas attack and then re-oiled. Oil cleaning will prevent corrosion for 12 hours or more, but the first available opportunity must be taken to dismantle machine guns and clean all parts in boiling water containing a little soda. If this is not done, corrosion continues slowly even after oil cleaning and may ultimately put the gun out of action.

After a gas attack, S.A.A. should be carefully examined. All rounds affected by gas must be replaced by new cartridges immediately and the old ones cleaned and expended as soon as possible.

76. All hand and rifle grenades exposed to the gas should have their safety-pins and working parts cleaned and re-oiled.

77. All bright parts of light trench mortars, together with all accessories and spare parts exposed to the gas, must be cleaned and wiped dry as soon as possible after the attack and in any case within 24 hours, after which they should be thoroughly coated afresh with oil. The same applies to ammunition which may have been exposed to the gas.

Ammunition which, for any reason, had not been oiled, must be cleaned and oiled and expended as soon as possible.

For details regarding the cleaning of guns and artillery ammunition and signal equipment, see paras. 116 and 123.

(v) TREATMENT OF SHELL HOLES.

78. In the neighbourhood of shelters or battery positions where gas from shell holes is causing annoyance, the holes and the ground round them should be covered with at least a foot of fresh earth. Shell holes so treated should not be disturbed, as the chemical is not thereby destroyed and only disappears slowly.

III.—PROTECTIVE APPLIANCES.

A.—INDIVIDUAL PROTECTIVE APPLIANCES.

(i) BOX RESPIRATOR.

(a) Description.

79. The box respirator consists of a box packed with chemicals and connected by means of a flexible rubber tube to an impervious face-piece or mask. The inspired air enters through a valve in the bottom of the box; the expired air is expelled through a valve just outside the face-piece. The wearer breathes in and out through a mouthpiece inside the mask, breathing through the nose being prevented by a nose-clip inserted in the face-piece. The latter is made of gas-proof fabric and is arranged to fit the face closely, being held in position by two elastic bands. As it encloses the eyes, the mask is fitted with two eyepieces which allow

a wide field of vision. These should be treated with anti-dimming composition, but if necessary they can be cleaned without removing the respirator, by means of folds in the material. The mouthpiece can be removed from the mouth to enable the wearer to speak, without disturbing the fit of the mask. The complete respirator is carried in a special satchel which is divided into two compartments, one of which holds the box and the other the mask. The box rests on a metal saddle which raises it from the bottom of the satchel and allows the free access of air.

(b) **Personal Fitting.**

80. It is necessary that each man should have a box respirator, the mask of which fits his face properly. For this reason the face-pieces are made in four sizes, which are issued in the following proportions.

   No. 1. Extra Small. Only issued on special indent.
   No. 2. Small. 10 per cent.
   No. 3. Medium. 80 per cent.
   No. 4. Large. 10 per cent.

The fit of each man's mask must be inspected and then tested in a gas chamber. Almost any room which can be closed up tightly may be used for this purpose, but the most suitable arrangement is to have a double door or a door and a curtain, similar to the protected dug-outs, so that as little of the gas as possible escapes into the outer air. A still better arrangement is to use two adjoining rooms, the inner of which is the actual gas chamber. A small quantity of lachrymatory liquid is sprayed into the room, and the man enters, wearing his box respirator. He must remain in the room five minutes and move about and talk. If the mask does not fit, lachrymation quickly ensues and the man retires. He should then be examined to see whether the lack of fit is due to bad adjustment or to his having a wrong size of mask. In the latter case a different size must be issued and the test repeated.

The fitting and adjusting of masks cannot be too thoroughly carried out. Special attention must be paid to the fitting of the mask and nose-clip with men who wear spectacles.

(c) **Method of Use.**

81. The satchel containing the box respirator is carried outside all other equipment. When away from the trenches, it may be worn slung over the right shoulder, but men in the trenches or proceeding thither must carry it slung on the chest as in the "Alert" position. The flap of the satchel with the press buttons must always be towards the body, but the press buttons must be kept fastened, except during an actual "Gas Alert." The method of wearing the box respirator and of putting it on from the "Alert" position are fully described in Appendix I. It is important that the methods therein described should be practised by all who are equipped with the box respirator, to ensure rapidity in adjustment and proper care in its use.

82. Men with perforated ear drums may be affected by the gas penetrating through the ear passages to the respiratory organs and causing irritation there. In these cases it is useful to plug the ears with wadding. C.O'.s should ascertain from the Medical Officers in charge of their units the names of those suffering from this disability in order that the above precaution may be taken.

83. It must be remembered that the box respirator can be worn in gas for many hours on end without losing its efficiency or causing any distress. It may be breathed through in drills for a period of a quarter of an hour per week for an indefinite time without impairing its efficiency. This permits a drill period of at least an hour per week. This is in addition to the initial drills referred to in Appendix I, amounting to 1½ hours breathing through the box.

84. (*d*) **Replacement. Record of use.**

The correct keeping of records as to hours of use of the box respirator, by entries in the small book forming part of the repair outfit, is a matter of the greatest importance, as these records form the only guide as to whether the boxes should or should not be replaced. Decision as to replacement should be made on the advice of the Divisional Gas Officer. The approximate time of actually breathing through the box should be noted. These entries must always be made after drills and gas attacks, great care being taken that they are correct.

(*e*) **Inspection.**

85. Box respirators must normally be inspected once a week and daily during " Gas Alert."

It is of the utmost importance that the inspection should be carried out regularly and with the greatest care. Any neglect in doing this may lead to loss of life.

The points to be attended to will be found in Appendix II.

(*f*) **Anti-Dimming Composition.**

86. At the weekly inspection and after every time the respirator is worn, the composition provided for the purpose will be put on the eyepieces in the manner described in Appendix II (p. 41).

(*g*) **Local Repairs.**

87. A small repair outfit, consisting of pieces of adhesive plaster is included, with a record card, in each satchel.

Small perforations in the face-pieces can be made good by applying pieces of the adhesive plaster to the perforation, both inside and outside the mask. They should be large enough to overlap the hole all round. Box respirators so repaired should be exchanged as soon as possible. The repair is only intended to make them safe until a new respirator can be obtained.

No other local repairs are permitted and all defective respirators must be handed in and new ones obtained.

Box respirators which have fallen into water must be exchanged as soon as possible.

(ii) P.H. HELMET.

(a) General.

88. The P.H. helmet is the reserve defence against a gas attack and great care must be taken by officers to ensure that it is in good order and that the men have been trained in its use. The main point to impress on them is that the chemically-treated material acts as a filter and that all air breathed into the lungs must pass through the flannelette. The helmet is, therefore, useless unless properly tucked in under the jacket. During its passage through the material of the helmet all poisonous gas is absorbed by the chemicals. These chemicals, however, would be gradually destroyed by the breath or by undue exposure to the air, and the helmet is, therefore, provided with a valve to breathe out through. The helmet should not be exposed unnecessarily to the air. It must be kept from exposure and wet and only removed from the wallet for inspection and drill.

(b) Method of use.

89. When the box-respirator is worn the P.H. helmet should hang perpendicularly downwards from the left shoulder, the sling passing under the belt. It must be over all other equipment. Care is necessary in folding it properly in the wallet in such a manner that the valve and eye-pieces are not damaged and that it can be put on in the quickest possible time. The method of folding is described in Appendix II.

90. If, for any reason, a man has to rely on a P.H. helmet for his anti-gas protection, he should wear it during "Gas Alert" periods in the manner prescribed in Appendix I. All equipment should be adjusted so that nothing interferes with the rapid putting on of the helmet.

(c) Drill.

91. **Helmet drill should be carried out frequently by all ranks.** It should aim at teaching the quick adjustment of helmets under all conditions, accustoming men to wearing them for a long time and taking exercise in them. Drill must be carried out both with and without greatcoats and equipment and by night as well as by day. The points to be attended to in helmet drill are specified in Appendix I.

(d) Inspection of Helmets.

92. Helmets must be inspected once a week and daily during "Gas Alert." It is of the utmost importance that this inspection should be carried out regularly and with the greatest care. Any neglect in doing this may lead to loss of life. The points to be attended to will be found in Appendix II.

(e) Replacement and Repair.

93. Helmets will be withdrawn as follows:—
   (1) Immediately after a cloud gas attack.
   (2) After being worn for a total period of 24 hours in gas shell bombardments, false gas attacks or drill.
   (3) After being carried for 28 days in the "Alert" position.

Slight defects, such as the cross-threading of eye-pieces, should be rectified locally with the help of the Company Gas N.C.O. Helmets the defects of which cannot immediately be rectified must be condemned.

(iii) ANTI-GAS GOGGLES.

94. Goggles for use against lachrymatory gas will be carried in the helmet satchel by all ranks. They will be inspected weekly, and treated with anti-dimming composition, in the manner described in Appendix II.

(iv) HORSE RESPIRATORS.

95. A full description of the Horse Respirator and the method of using it is given in Appendix III.

B.—ANTI-GAS APPLIANCES FOR GENERAL USE.

(i) STROMBOS HORNS.

(a) General.

96. The experience gained in recent gas attacks has shown that Strombos Horns are the most effective form of gas alarm appliance and are audible for very long distances.

(b) Description.

97. Each horn is issued in a box containing one horn, two compressed-air cylinders, one length of rubber tubing with screw connections, one screwdriver, one gimlet and one adjustable spanner. One spare cylinder is issued with the horn, to be kept at the Divisional or Brigade H.Q. to replace used cylinders without delay. A reserve of charged cylinders is also kept at the Heavy Mobile Workshop.

(c) **Method of Use.**

98. The horn should be mounted in a horizontal position by screwing to the outside of the case or to some other suitable support and must be protected as much as possible from rain or shell splinters. Should it be necessary to change its position, the horn should be fixed in the box by means of the butterfly nuts provided. Strombos horns must always be ready for use, the horn being connected to one of the compressed-air cylinders by the rubber tube. The union joints at both ends of the tube must be tight.

99. **To sound the horn, unscrew the screw cap on the air cylinder two complete turns.** The horn will sound for about one minute.

Immediately after use, couple up the horn to the second air cylinder and leave it ready for use in case of a second gas cloud. The used cylinder should be clearly marked EMPTY and replaced as soon as possible from the reserve.

(d) **Replacement and Repair.**

100. The pressure of the cylinders will be tested under arrangements made by the Divisional Gas Officer once every week and defective ones returned through D.A.D.O.S. for re-charging at the Heavy Mobile Workshop.

On no account is any adjustment of the horn to be attempted except by the Divisional Gas Officer or his trained Divisional Gas N.C.Os. A horn will be thrown completely out of action by movement of any of its parts.

Damaged horns must be sent to the Army Heavy Mobile Workshop for repairs.

(ii) OTHER GAS ALARM DEVICES.

101. No definite pattern has been adopted for secondary alarm devices suitable for installing at every sentry post. Bells, gongs (shell cases), suspended rails and other appliances are all in use, but single bells and gongs are generally too weak and all of these arrangements suffer from requiring the use of a man's hands.

A very suitable arrangement as an alarm is a triangle of light steel rail, mounted in such a way that it can be beaten by working a treadle. It can thus be sounded by a sentry while he is putting on his respirator or helmet. Similar devices not requiring the use of the hands should be devised and installed where possible.

(iii) ANTI-GAS FANS.

102. The Anti-gas Fan consists of a sheet of canvas supported by braces of cane and re-inforced in the middle. It is made with

two transverse hinges and is fitted with a hickory handle. The flapping portion is roughly 15 inches square and the handle is 2 feet long.

Method of Use.

(a) Clearing Trenches.

103. The fan blade is placed on the ground with the brace side *downwards*, the man using it being in a slightly crouching position with the left foot advanced, the right hand grasping the handle at the neck and the left hand near the butt end. The fan is brought up quickly over the right shoulder, and then smartly flicked to the ground with quick slapping strokes. This drives a current of air along the earth and, on the top strokes, throws the gas out of the trench as it were by a shovel.

It is essential that the part of the fan blade nearest the handle should touch the ground first, and this can be accomplished in all cases by ending the stroke with the whole length of the handle as close to the ground as possible.

104. In working round a traverse, &c., the fan should be flapped round the corner with the hinge on the corner and the lower edge of the fan as near the bottom of the trench as can be managed. The brace side of the fan is to be outwards and at the end of the stroke the whole length of the handle should be close up to the side of the trench.

If several fans are available, men should work in single file and with " out-of-step " strokes, *i.e.*, one fan should be up while the next is down.

(b) Clearing Shelters.

105. In the case of a dug-out with a single entrance not exceeding 12 feet in length, the gas is first cleared from the neighbourhood of the shelter as in 103 and then the corners worked round as in 104. The worker now advances to the inner end of the entrance, beating rather slowly on the ground to allow the gas time to get out of the tunnel and bringing the fan as near the roof as possible on the return stroke.

It may be desirable to have a second fan working just outside the dug-out to throw the gas out of the trench as it comes out.

106. In the case of dug-outs with two entrances or with one entrance and another opening, such as a chimney, it is only necessary to use the fan round the corner of one entrance in the manner described in 104. When the entrance is cleared, it is advisable to enter the shelter with a respirator on in order to beat up the gas from the floor boards, &c. This greatly facilitates the removal of the last traces of gas.

(iv) VERMOREL SPRAYERS.

107. Vermorel sprayers are withdrawn from general use for clearing out gas after an attack, but a certain number are retained for moistening the blankets of protected shelters and for use in medical dug-outs, &c. They should be kept for this purpose only and on no account relied on for clearing trenches or shelters of gas.

108. **Company Vermorel Sprayers.**—Sprayers on the basis of two per Company are retained for moistening blanket protection. They should be kept by Company Gas N.C.O.'s with other anti-gas trench stores, and should be kept one-third full of water. The solution must be kept in corked rum jars or other closed receptacles close to each sprayer; it must not be kept in the sprayers owing to its corrosive nature. It is made up as follows :—

> Water, 3 gallons (one large bucket).
> Sodium Thiosulphate (hypo.), $1\frac{1}{2}$ lbs. ($\frac{3}{4}$ mess-tin).
> Sodium Carbonate (washing soda), 3 lbs. ($1\frac{1}{2}$ mess-tins).

Three rum jars are required to hold the above quantity and the necessity for keeping them corked must be impressed on the personnel responsible for it.

When no solution is obtainable, water may be used for spraying the blankets.

(v) GAS SAMPLING APPARATUS.

109. It is very desirable that samples be obtained of the enemy gas used in attacks, especially cloud gas attacks. For this purpose two kinds of appliances are kept in the trenches, viz., Vacuum Bulbs and Gas-testing Tubes. These should be looked after by the Company Gas N.C.O.'s, whose duty it is to take the samples, but officers should take all possible steps to ensure that samples of the gas are actually taken, as the information obtained may be of the greatest importance.

Full details of the methods of taking samples are laid down in "Standing Orders for Company Gas N.C.O.'s" (Appendix VII.).

IV.—CONSIDERATIONS AFFECTING SPECIAL ARMS.

110. The foregoing notes apply to all arms and are complete as regards considerations of gas defence affecting troops in trenches generally. Additional information for the guidance of other arms on anti-gas measures which affect them specially is given below.

(A).—CAVALRY.

111. It is unlikely that Cavalry, when mounted, will encounter high concentrations of gas from a gas cloud, or even from gas shells. It will probably be found therefore that, when acting as mounted troops, the P.H. helmet will be adequate protection, besides being less cumbersome for troops depending on their mobility.

112. On the other hand, Cavalry used to supplement Infantry in the line, or employed as working parties in or near the trenches, must be equipped for gas defence in the same way as other arms. In this case, it is impossible to wear the bandolier over the shoulder when the box respirator is worn in the "Alert" position. During the Gas Alert period, mounted troops must therefore wear the bandolier round the waist. This can be accomplished as follows (Fig. 1):—

113. (1) Unfasten the buckle D.

(2) Pull out strap A from the metal triangle C.

(3) Pass the bandolier round the waist.

(4) Pass strap A from behind forwards through the aperture E, situated under pouch H. (This aperture may have to be slightly enlarged.)

(5) Pull on strap A until the bandolier fits and buckle off to D.

(6) Strap B1, with the attached buckle B, and triangle C, can now be tucked away under the bandolier to the right, behind pouches H and M.

(7) For thin subjects, it may be better to pass strap A through the aperture F between pouches H and M before buckling it off to D, so as to make the bandolier tighter.

(B).—ARTILLERY.

(i) GENERAL.

114. Artillery are probably more liable than anyone else to bombardment with gas shells, both poisonous and lachrymatory. Owing to the suddenness of shell attacks and the long period that the neighbourhood of a battery may be affected by lachrymators, it is essential that the following points be noted:—

(a) Where, owing to circumstances, box respirators are not actually worn on the man, they must be hung separately

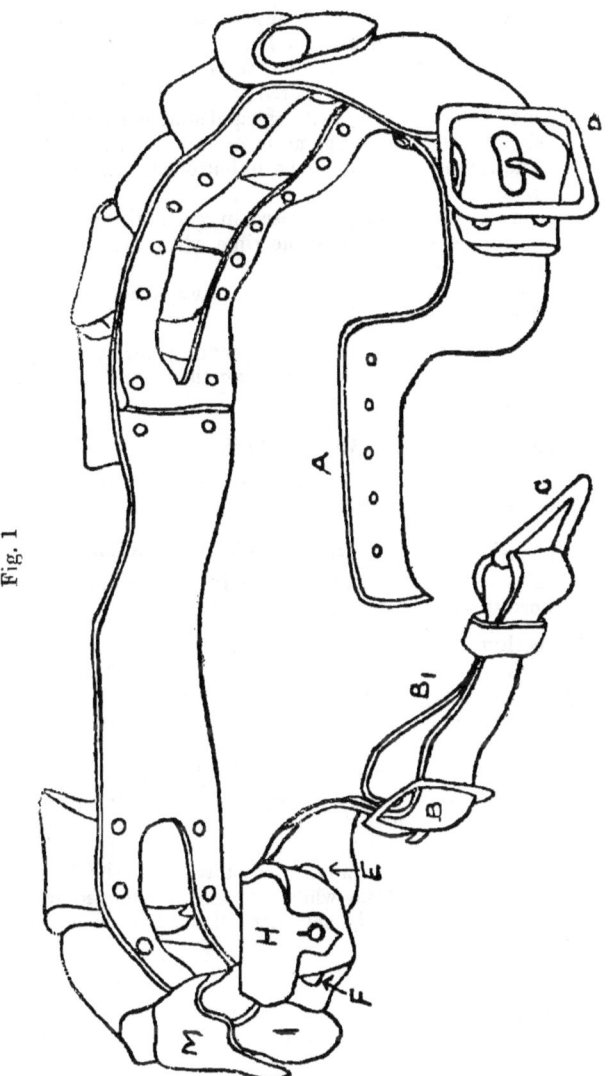

Fig. 1

and within easy reach of the owners. (They should not, if possible, be hung in the actual gun emplacements, owing to the concussion being liable to displace the chemicals in the box.) If this course has to be adopted, the respirators should be ready prepared with the haversack sling shortened by means of the tab and stud and the slack of the sling tucked under the mask as in the " Alert " position. The satchel flap should be unbuttoned, but kept in position.

Men must be thoroughly practised in getting their respirators on in the shortest possible time when they are stored in this manner.

The P.H. helmet will, in any case, always be carried on the man in case of emergency.

(b) **Men must be** well practised in wearing their box respirators for long periods and in serving their guns while wearing respirators or anti-gas goggles.

(ii) FORWARD OBSERVING PARTIES.

115. Forward observing parties must take all the precautions previously laid down for Infantry.

(iii) PRESERVATION OF GUNS AND AMMUNITION.

116. The following precautions apply to medium and heavy trench mortars as well as to guns and howitzers:

(a) Protection.

Batteries which are in constant danger of gas attacks, whether from gas clouds or gas shells, should keep all bright parts of the gun or mortar, carriage, mounting and accessories well coated with oil.

Sights and all instruments should also be smeared with oil and protected with covers when not in actual use, care being taken that the oil does not come in contact with any glass or find its way into the interior of the instrument.

Cartridge cases of the ammunition stored with the Battery and all uncapped fuses, or fuses which have been removed from their cylinders, should be wiped over with oil as soon as possible and protected with a cover.

(b) Cleaning.

All bright parts of guns and trench mortars, together with all accessories and spare parts exposed to the gas, must be cleaned and wiped dry as soon as possible after the attack, and in any case within 24 hours, after which they should be thoroughly coated afresh with oil.

The same applies to the whole of the ammunition still in the Battery position. Ammunition which, for any reason, had not been oiled, must be cleaned and oiled. It is desirable to expend it as soon as possible.

(iv) AIMING POINTS AND AIMING POSTS.

117. Aiming points and aiming posts are liable to be obscured by the gas cloud and arrangements should, therefore, be made in every Battery to meet this eventuality by providing gun-pits with means to check the line of fire if necessary, without depending on the use of aiming posts.

(v) TACTICAL MEASURES DURING A GAS ATTACK.

118. Enemy gas attacks may be executed for purposes other than the preparation of a subsequent infantry attack. During the gas discharge a heavy artillery fire on the actual trenches whence the gas is issuing is the best way of dealing with the situation. Also t is essential that the gas discharge should be interfered with **as early as possible**, as the opening periods of the discharge are the most effective.

119. To ensure an effective and immediate artillery fire the following points require attention :—

(a) Certain howitzer Batteries should be detailed to open a rapid fire for a short time as an anti-gas measure.

(b) Only certain portions of the enemy's front trenches can be used for gas discharge in any given wind and these can easily be indicated on any accurate trench map. Each Battery charged with the task of hampering an enemy gas attack should be provided with a map and a table, showing from what portions of the enemy's lines (within the Battery's zone of action) gas can be discharged in any given wind.

120. Nothing in the foregoing paragraphs in any way affects the responsibility of artillery for dealing with any infantry attack, or for the execution of counter-battery work.

(C).—TUNNELLING COMPANIES.

121 (i) Tunnelling companies are again reminded that neither the box respirator nor the P.H. helmet affords protection against mine or explosion gases.

(ii) Owing to the difficulty in clearing gas, especially lachrymatory gas, from mine-shafts and galleries, the entrances to mine-shafts should be protected from gas by blanket curtains in the manner already described for dug-outs.

(iii) The enemy has occasionally attempted to render our galleries untenable by the use of lachrymatory bombs in conjunction with the explosion of a charge. If this is done, goggles will generally be found sufficient protection; but if the concentration is so high as to affect the nose or lungs, the box respirator must be worn if work has to be continued.

(D).—SIGNAL SERVICE AND TELEPHONE OPERATORS.

(i) GENERAL.

122. It is essential that telephone operators should be able to work as much as possible during a gas attack without wearing respirators or helmets. Signal dug-outs must, therefore, be particularly carefully protected against gas, so as to allow this to be done.

(ii) Telephone operators must be specially practised in using their instruments when wearing box respirators or helmets. The headpiece of the receiver will be worn over the helmet. The buzzer should be used when the respirator or helmet is worn.

(iii) Linesmen must receive plenty of practice in carrying on their work, both at night and in the day-time, while wearing box respirators and also goggles.

(ii) PRESERVATION OF SIGNAL EQUIPMENT.

(a) Protection of Telephone Instruments.

123. The only effective method of preventing corrosion of electrical apparatus during a gas attack is to prevent the gas reaching it and the best way of doing this is to have Signal Shelters and Offices thoroughly protected against gas. As the corrosive effect on damp instruments is very much greater than on dry instruments, the shelters should be kept as dry as possible.

During a gas attack, D. Mk. III. telephones must be kept in their leather cases and unless the buzzer key is being used the leather flap must be kept down, leaving only the cords with receiver and hand-set out of the case. The backs of switchboards and buzzer exchanges must be kept closed. All apparatus, such as magneto telephones, test boards, spare instruments, &c., which it is not essential to have uncovered should be well covered up with cloths, blankets or coats, &c.

(b) Cleaning Instruments after a Gas Attack.

124. After a gas attack, telephone apparatus that has been exposed to gas should be treated as follows:—

The ends of the wires should be removed from terminals and

cleaned by being scraped with a knife, wiped with a damp cloth and dried. Terminals, exchange plugs and all exposed metal work should be cleaned first with a damp and then with a dry cloth. This process should be repeated after 12 hours have elapsed. The metal work of the leather case of the D. Mk. III. telephone and of other instrument cases should be cleaned with oil in the same way as rifles, &c. The internal portions of the instruments should not be interfered with. If an instrument has been kept closed or covered up, it is very unlikely that internal portions will have suffered; but if these portions show signs of corrosion, the instruments should be sent back to Division or Corps Headquarters to be dealt with by an Instrument Repairer.

(iii) PROTECTION OF CARRIER PIGEONS.

125. When the gas alarm is sounded, all baskets containing pigeons should be placed in the special Anti-Gas Bags provided for this purpose, or placed in gas-proof shelters. If for any reason the birds cannot be protected from the gas, they should be liberated at once. Anti-gas bags should always be kept near baskets containing birds, and should be regularly inspected.

Pigeons can be utilised during a gas attack. Experience has proved that they will fly through any gas cloud, but it is imperative that the bird should be exposed to the gas for as short a time as possible. The message and carrier should, therefore, be prepared and if possible, fastened to the pigeon's leg, before the bird is exposed to the gas. Twenty seconds should suffice to fix a carrier and liberate a bird.

LIST OF APPENDICES.

I. Drills with Box Respirators and Helmets.

II. Inspection of Personal Anti-gas Equipment.

III. Instructions for the Use of Horse Respirators.

IV. Typical Standing Orders for Action during Gas Alert and Hostile Gas Attacks.

V. Typical Standing Orders for Company Gas N.C.O's.

VI. Instructions for Making Wind Observations and Furnishing Reports.

VII. Instructions for taking Gas Samples and for Reporting on Hostile Gas Attacks.

APPENDIX I.

DRILLS WITH BOX RESPIRATORS AND TUBE HELMETS.

1.—Box Respirators.

Practices " A " and " B " will be carried out twice weekly, when there is no gas alert on. Practice " B " will be carried out once daily during the gas alert period, the actual time during which the box is breathed through being as short as possible.

Practices " C," " E " and " F " will be carried out occasionally.

Practices " D," " G " and " H " will be carried out as frequently as possible having regard to the amount of time during which the box may be breathed through.

In the initial training drills must be so arranged that every man wears the respirator for one full period of half-an-hour without removing the mask or noseclip.

Time during which box may be breathed through for drill purposes.

    During initial training ... For 1½ hours, giving 6 to 7 hours' drill.

    Subsequently ... For ¼ hour weekly, giving 1 hour's drill.

Practice " A."

Adjustment of the Box Respirator in the " Alert " position.

On the command " Gas Alert," hang the box respirator round the neck with the press buttons next the body. With the right hand seize the satchel by the leather tab, with the left hand seize the sling by the brass button and clip this into the leather tab. Undo the press buttons, closing the satchel.

The length of whipcord will then be withdrawn from the right-hand compartment, passed through the ring on the right of the satchel and carried round the waist to the ring on the left, where it is fastened. The press buttons closing the satchel will be left undone, but the flap will be put in position to keep the respirator from wet.

Practice " B."

Drill " by numbers " to obtain correct adjustment of the Box Respirator.

NOTE—This drill is to be carried out alternately with one " judging the time," *i.e.*, as quick adjustment as possible. It is the most important and complete adjustment must be obtained by all ranks in SIX SECONDS.

Adjust the respirator in the alert position with satchel covered but not buttoned.

1. On the command " One " press down both thumbs between the satchel and the body and open the satchel flap. Immediately seize the mask with the right hand, the metal elbow tube just outside the mask being in the palm of the hand and the thumb and first finger grasping the wire frame of the nose clip.

2. On the command " Two " bring the mask smartly out of the satchel and hold it in both hands with all the fingers outside round the binding and the two thumbs inside, pointing inwards and upwards under the elastic. At the same time *throw the chin well forward* ready to enter the mask opposite the nose clip.

3. On the command " Three " bring the mask forward, digging the chin into it and with the same motion bringing the elastic bands back over

the crown of the head to the full extent of the retaining tape, using the thumbs.

4. On the command "Four" seize the metal elbow tube outside the mask, thumb on the right, fingers on the left—all pointing towards the face. Push the rubber mouthpiece well into the mouth and pull it forward until the rim of the mouthpiece lies between the teeth and the lips and the two rubber grips are held by the teeth.

5. On the command "Five" adjust the nose-clip to the nose, using the thumb and first three fingers of the right hand. Run the fingers round the mask on either side of the face to make sure that the edges are not folded over. Correct any faults in adjustment. Come smartly to attention.

Practice "C."

To adjust Box Respirators when carried over the shoulder and not in Alert position.

Sling the satchel round so that it hangs in front of the body. Undo the press buttons and adjust the mask as in Practice "B," allowing the satchel to hang by the rubber tube.

After the noseclip is put on, at once proceed to adjust the satchel in the Alert position, as in practice "A."

Practice "D."

Drill to teach cleaning of eyepieces.

On the command "Clean Eyepieces" the right eyepiece will be gripped between the thumb and first finger of the left hand. The first finger of the right hand will then be pushed gently into the fold of the mask behind the right eyepiece which will be cleaned with a gentle circular motion.

The left eyepiece will be cleaned in a similar way.

Practice "E."

Drill to teach method of giving orders.

It is first explained to a squad that the noseclip must not be removed to talk and that before each sentence is spoken a long breath must be taken and the mouthpiece removed sideways from the mouth by turning the metal tube outside the mask to one side. After speaking, the mouthpiece is replaced.

The squad should then be numbered off, extended to four paces, and orders passed along the line.

Officers and N.C.Os. will receive special care in Practice "E."

Practice "F."

Drill to teach method of clearing mask from gas which may have leaked in and is affecting the eyes.

Press the mask close to the face, forcing out foul air round the sides and then fill again with fresh air from the lungs by blowing out round the mouthpiece.

Practice "G."

Drill to teach method of testing whether trench or dug-out is free from gas.

With the right hand open the facepiece away from the right cheek, then loosen the nose clip on the nose and smell gently (do not take a breath). If gas is smelt, the nose clip and mask are replaced. Then as in Drill "**F**"

Practice " H."

Ordinary infantry drill will be carried out while wearing the mask. This will include doubling for at least 200 yards at a time. Marching order will be worn. Musketry and bombing instruction and training of specialists (including artillery, machine gunners, signallers, R.A.M.C.) will also be carried out.

Practice " I."

Drill to teach changing from the box respirator to the tube helmet. (To be carried out with collar and top button undone.)

On the command " Change " **hold the breath**, get out the tube helmet and grip in the left hand with the fingers inside the opening. Knock off the steel helmet with the right hand. Thrust the right hand from behind underneath the sling of satchel, inserting the fingers underneath the mask at chin. Bending forward, pull sling over head and mask off in one movement. Get on the tube helmet, and when the chin grip is obtained commence breathing again.

Protection must be obtained in TEN SECONDS or less.

NOTE.—(a) If after wearing for a long time, the pressure of the nose clip becomes unbearable, it may be relieved for a few moments by taking off the pressure without removing clip.

(b) Removing masks. It must be seen that when masks are removed, this is done without strain on the facepiece or elastic. On the command " Take off masks " insert the fingers of the left hand under the mask at the chin, bend the head forward, at the same time removing the mask with an *upward* motion of the left hand.

(c) After all drill the mask must be *wiped dry*, folded correctly, and put away in such a way that the rubber valve is not bent.

2.—Tube Helmet Drill.

Helmet drill should be carried out frequently by all ranks. It should aim at teaching the quick adjustment of helmets under all conditions, accustoming men to wearing them for a long time and taking exercise in them. Drill must be carried out both with and without greatcoats and equipment and by night as well as by day.

Men may use their own helmets for drill purposes. Tube helmets which have been worn for 24 hours for drill will be replaced.

The following points are to be noted:—

(i) Men must be timed against a watch in removing the helmet from its wallet, getting it over the head and gripped at the neck with one hand so that the material is tight all round. This should take less than 6 seconds and the importance of continual carrying out of this practice cannot be too strongly emphasised. Men should be taught to **hold the breath** while putting on the helmet, as a few breaths drawn in concentrated gas may be followed by serious results. The remainder of the adjustment is to be completed with the free hand before the hand below the chin is removed. Officers should turn up the collars of their jackets after the skirt of the helmet has been tucked in, fixing them in front by means of a safety pin carried for the purpose or by a special button. Many cases of "gassing" have been caused by helmets not being tucked in properly under the jacket. It is desirable for all ranks to turn up their collars after completing the adjustment.

(ii) It must be seen that every man is breathing out through the valve.

(iii) Men must be warned that during a gas attack the smell of the chemical on the helmet becomes stronger and causes slight irritation of the eyes, nose and throat and that this smell does not indicate that the gas is coming through the helmet.

(iv) Men must be taught that misty eyepieces can be cleared by rubbing them against the forehead.

Gas Alert Position.

If, for any reason a man has only a P.H. helmet for use as anti-gas protection, he should wear it as follows during the alert period:—

(1) Put the helmet on in the usual way. Pin the front edge of the helmet and the top edge of the opened wallet to the shirt with two safety pins in such a manner that the helmet may be readily pulled on and off the head without removing the pins, the wallet hanging loose below it.

(2) Leaving the safety pins in position, remove the helmet and fold the sides over the eyepieces to the usual width, keeping the valve horizontal and flat. Now roll up the helmet and tuck it inside the jacket. Cover with the wallet by pulling up the latter so that it lies in front of the helmet and button up the jacket with the exception of the two upper buttons.

(3) On the gas alarm sounding, open the coat so that the helmet falls, pull the latter over the head and adjust in the usual manner. Quick adjustment is essential, and the "chin grip" should be obtained in two seconds. The wallet hangs suspended by the pins and is ready for use if required.

All equipment should be adjusted so as not to interfere with the quick putting on of the helmet, *e.g.*, nothing should be slung across the chest.

General Points on Training with Anti-Gas Appliances.

When training men in the use of anti-gas appliances the following points are of importance. They apply equally to box respirators and P.H. helmets:—

(a) Practice in simple movements in box respirators or helmets. Ordinary infantry drill should be combined with physical drill, including arm and leg exercises, leap-frog and doubling. The time of practice should not exceed 15 minutes at first, and should be gradually extended in the case of the P.H. helmet.

(b) Practice in bombing, rapid loading and aiming, judging distance and range practice, should be carried out while men are wearing box respirators or helmets.

(c) Men must swallow their saliva and not allow it to drain out over the lips or through the valve.

(d) Officers and N.C.Os. will receive the same training as the men and in addition will be practised in giving orders whilst wearing their respirators or helmets.

Practice and drill in the use of anti-gas appliances should be carried out continuously. This applies especially to troops which have returned to trench warfare after having been in districts where more open fighting may have led (a) to a temporary lapse in this training, (b) to the subsequent incorporation of drafts only partially trained in anti-gas measures.

APPENDIX II.

INSPECTION OF PERSONAL ANTI-GAS EQUIPMENT.

A.—Box Respirators.

Box respirators must normally be inspected once a week and daily during "Gas Alert." Attention will be paid to the following points :—

(a) Boxes, facepiece, mouthpiece, noseclip, eyepieces and elastic must be in good order. If the box is rusted through the respirator must be condemned.

(b) Facepiece must be firmly attached to the mouthpiece and to the elbow tube.

(c) The metal tube inside the mouthpiece must be about $\frac{1}{8}$-in. back from the opening of the latter.

(d) The rubber tube must be intact and firmly attached to the box and elbow tube.

(e) The expiratory valve should be tested by removing the box from the satchel and either closing the cap at the bottom with the hand, or pinching the rubber tube so as to prevent inlet of air at the same time attempting to draw in air through the mouthpiece. It should not be possible to draw in any air. This also proves the absence of leaks in the tube or box. It must be possible to breathe out easily through the valve. If the latter has stuck because of saliva drying in it, this must be remedied by rubbing the valve between the fingers.

(f) See that the inlet valve is opening properly and that air can be drawn freely through the box.

(g) See that the whipcord is present and not knotted.

(h) Any small perforations in the facepiece should be temporarily repaired by applying pieces of adhesive plaster from the repair outfit to the perforation, both inside and outside the mask. The adhesive plaster should be large enough to overlap the hole all round.

Respirators so repaired must be exchanged as soon as possible.

(*i*) Replace the box in the satchel so that the facepiece comes to the face without twist on the tube. Fold facepiece carefully and replace in the satchel so that the expiratory valve is not likely to crumple.

B.—P.H. Helmets

Helmets must be inspected once a week, or daily during "Gas Alert." Attention must be paid to the following points:—

(*a*) See that the satchel and wallet are in good order.

(*b*) Folding. See that the helmet is properly folded with the valve flat, and no strain on the flannelette round the valve seating.

The folding should be done as follows:—

Hold the helmet under the chin with the eyepieces away from the body.

Arrange the valve so that it lies flat pointing to the right (Fig. 2).

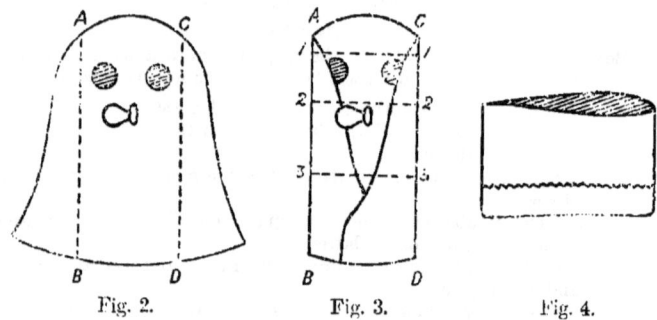

Fig. 2.   Fig. 3.   Fig. 4.

Fold the right hand edge of the helmet forward along AB, arranging the valve to lie flat on top of the fold. Then fold the left-hand edge forward along CD (Fig. 3).

Fold over top along line 1.1, then along line 2.2, and finally along 3.3.

The skirt should be now folded over and the folded helmet should appear as in Fig. 4. This should now be placed in the wallet with the skirt next to the flap side of the wallet.

(*c*) Valves. The two parts of the valve screw together. The joint should be tight and should grip the flannelette. The mouthpiece should be horizontal. See that the rubber valve is fastened securely to the metal. Each man must test the valve of his helmet by breathing through it. He should not be able to breathe IN easily through the valve. The valve rubber sometimes becomes hard. This can be remedied by breathing out through the valve for about a minute at each helmet inspection.

(d) Eyepieces. These should be screwed up tightly from the inside and should grip the flannelette. Screw threads must not be crossed. The glasses must not be cracked or loose.

(e) There must not be the smallest hole through which gas might enter. Particular attention must be paid to the flannelette round the eyepieces and valve seating.

(f) If helmets become so sodden with water that it is impossible to breathe through them, they must then be condemned.

C.—Anti-Gas Goggles.

Goggles must be inspected weekly and the following points specially noted :—

(a) The windows should be unbroken.

(b) Elastic or tapes must be in good condition.

Treatment with Anti-Dimming Composition.

After each inspection the windows should be treated afresh with Anti-dimming Composition. This should be done as follows : Apply a little of the paste with a dry rag to the inside of the eyepiece, rubbing it hard into the glass or film. Then polish off as much as possible with a dry rag, leaving the glass quite clear. This process must be repeated after each time that goggles have been worn.

APPENDIX III.

DIRECTIONS FOR THE USE OF ANTI-GAS HORSE RESPIRATOR.

1.—Description.

The respirator consists of a flannelette bag with a canvas mouthpiece which goes into the horse's mouth and saves the flannelette from being bitten through. The bag is provided with an elastic band which passes round the opening so as to draw the respirator close to the face when in use. The upper side of the mouth of the flannelette bag is furnished with a small unbleached calico patch by which the respirator is attached to the nose band of the head collar when in the "alert" position, and while in use. Inside the bag and attached to the canvas mouthpiece there is a canvas frame which is stitched on to the bag in such a way as to prevent the material drawing into the nostrils when the respirator is in use. The whole is folded and carried in a canvas case provided with a flap, secured by three press buttons, and having two straps at the back by which the case is attached to the head collar.

2.—Method of Use.

Horses can stand a higher concentration of gas than human beings without material damage, and it is not therefore necessary to protect them against cloud gas attacks when they are a considerable distance back from the trenches. Nor is it necessary to protect their eyes. The respirator is primarily intended for use on transport animals when they are sent to the vicinity of the trenches with supplies, ammunition, &c. In the case of gas shell attacks, horses should be protected wherever the shelling is heavy.

(i) **Carrying when not Immediately Required.**

When not required for immediate use the respirator can be conveniently carried on the supporting strap of the breast harness as shown in Fig. 5, or if a zinc wither pad is worn, still more conveniently inside this pad. However carried, the case is steadied by being strapped on either side to the metal ring on the supporting strap, and its flap should be passed under this strap, between it and the numnah wither pad, and buttoned as in the " alert " position.

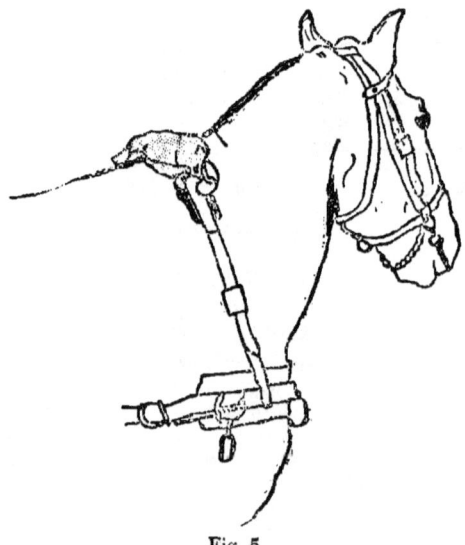

Fig. 5.

(ii) **Alert Position.**

When horses are being sent up to the trenches, the transport or other officer responsible should have the respirators adjusted in the "alert" position before moving off, as follows:—

    (*a*) The flap of the respirator case is unbuttoned and slipped under the nose-band of the head collar from below upwards.

    (*b*) The two straps at the back are also passed under the nose band and secured to the cheek pieces of the head collar, above the metal D on each side.

(c) The small unbleached calico patch on the upper side of the mouth of the respirator is buttoned on to the noseband of the head collar so that the respirator is ready to be slipped on immediately in the event of a gas attack.

(d) The cover of the case is then closed over the nose band, and the respirator is thus protected from rain, &c., and held in position on the nose band. Fig. 6 shows a respirator in its case carried in the "alert" position.

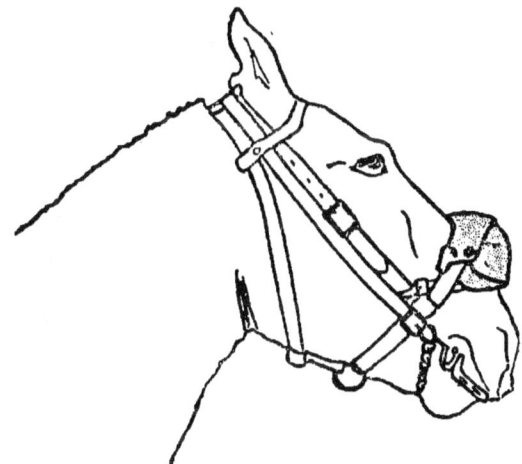

Fig. 6.

(iii) **Wearing in Gas.**

The respirator being carried in the "alert" position is adjusted for use as follows :—

(a) The flap of the case is unbuttoned and the respirator removed, leaving the case attached to the check pieces of the head collar and lying flat on the face.

(b) The mouth of the bag is drawn down over the upper lip and upper teeth with one hand on each side of the mouthpiece, slipped into the mouth, and drawn well up to the angle of the lips.

(c) The elastic band is seized on either side close to the mouthpiece and pulled outwards so as to draw the mouth of the bag tight around the upper jaw, above the nostrils, and is then slipped over the poll.

The respirator is then in position and the animal may be worked in it without difficulty or undue distress. The bit and reins are not interfered with in any way. This is shown in Fig. 7.

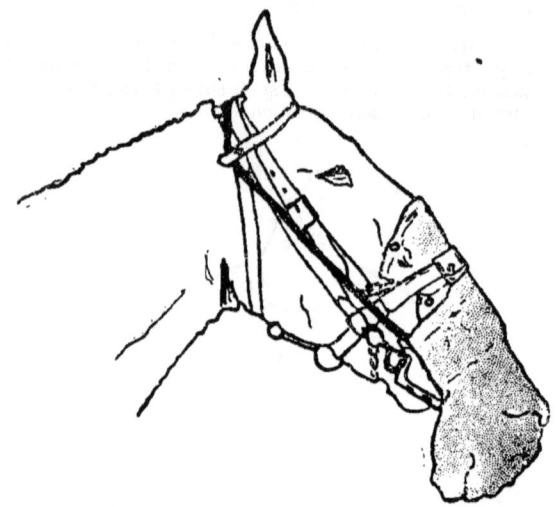

Fig. 7.

(iv) Replacement in Case.

In folding the respirator and replacing it in the case ready for use the following points should be observed:—

(a) The canvas mouthpiece should be wiped as clean as possible.

(b) The flannelette bag should be held with the canvas mouthpiece underneath and the elastic band placed over the top of the bag in such a way that when the canvas patch is buttoned on to the nose band the elastic band has simply to be passed straight up over the face and over the poll. The bottom end of the respirator should then be tucked in and rolled up over the elastic band to make a neat roll for insertion in the canvas case.

APPENDIX IV.

TYPICAL STANDING ORDERS FOR ACTION DURING GAS ALERT AND HOSTILE GAS ATTACKS.

NOTE.—*These are Specimen Orders for guidance of Commanders in Drawing up their own Orders.*

1.—Ordering of Gas Alert.

Gas alert will be ordered when the wind is in the dangerous quarter, no matter what the strength of the wind.

The order "Gas Alert" will be sent out to all units by Corps H.Q. (or, if authority has been so delegated, by Divisional H.Q.), but Brigade H.Q. or Battalion Commanders are empowered to order a "Gas Alert" as a result of wind observations made by Company Gas N.C.Os. forwarded by Company Commanders. Such action will be reported immediately to the next higher formation.

"Gas Alert" will not be taken off without the authority of the Corps Commander, or the Divisional Commander to whom authority has been delegated.

2.—Behaviour During Gas Alert.

Inspection of Box Respirators and Helmets.

(i) All box respirators and helmets will be carefully inspected and the inspection repeated daily.

Alert Position for Box Respirators.

(ii) All ranks within one mile of the front line will carry their box respirators in the alert position. Nothing slung across the chest must interfere with the immediate use of the respirator.

Special Orders for men using P.H. Helmets.

(iii) The helmet will be carried in the alert position, *i.e.*, pinned through the wallet on to the shirt and rolled in such a manner as to protect the valve and leave the helmet suspended ready to put on the moment the jacket is opened.

(iv) The two upper buttons of both jacket and greatcoat will be left undone. Men are forbidden to wear mackintosh sheets round their shoulders, or mufflers round their necks.

(v) In no circumstances will anything (rifle, field glasses, &c.) be slung across the chest in such a manner as to interfere with the rapid adjustment of the helmet.

(vi) Jackets will not be taken off within one mile of the front line.

(vii) Officers and N.C.Os. in charge of any unit or party must see that the orders (i) to (vi) are strictly carried out, both for troops in front line trenches and for detached bodies of troops (working and carrying parties, &c.).

Sentries, &c.

(viii) All working parties will have a sentry posted to give instant warning of a gas attack.

(ix) A sentry will be posted at each Strombos Horn or other alarm device and instructed in its use.

(x) A sentry will be posted to every large dug-out and to each group of small dug-outs.

(xi) A sentry will be posted to each Headquarters, Signal Office and independent body of men.

(xii) Arrangements will be made by the officer in charge of the trench for warning the Artillery Observation Post if there is one in the trench.

(xiii) Commanders of units in billets within eight miles of the front line trenches will organise a system of giving the alarm and rousing all men in cellars or houses.

(xiv) At night sentries must have at least two men within reach of them so that the alarm can be spread rapidly.

Sleeping.

(xv) When a gas attack is probable, men in front line trenches will sleep on the fire-step instead of in dug-outs.

(xvi) Men sleeping in rearward lines or in works where they are allowed to take off their equipment, will sleep with their box respirators on the person.

Company Gas N.C.Os.

(xvii) Company Gas N.C.Os. will report to Company H.Q. in readiness to assist the Company Commander should a gas attack occur.

Ammonia Capsules.

(xviii) Medical Officers i/c units must see that a proper proportion of the ammonia capsules are with stretcher bearers in the front line, in readiness for their immediate use after a gas attack.

3.—Gas Alarm.

(i) In the event of an enemy gas attack the alarm will at once be given by all means available—by telephone, Strombos Horns, gongs and, if necessary, by orderly. Sentries will warn all ranks in trenches, dug-outs, observation posts or mine-shafts.

(ii) All ranks will at once put on their box respirators or helmets.

(iii) Troops in the front line trenches and elsewhere where the tactical situation requires it, will stand to arms. All ranks in the front lines are forbidden to remain in, or go into, dug-outs or move to a flank or to the rear.

(iv) If troops in support or reserve lines of trenches remain in, or go into, unprotected dug-outs, they must continue to wear their anti-gas appliances.

Unnecessary Movement to Cease.

(v) There must be as little movement and talking as possible.

(vi) On the alarm being given, all bodies of troops or transport on the move will halt and all working parties cease work until the gas cloud has passed.

(vii) If a relief is going on, units should stand steady as far as possible until the gas cloud has passed.

(viii) Supports and parties bringing up ammunition and grenades will only be moved up if the tactical situation demands.

Protected Shelters.

(ix) The blanket doorways of protected dug-outs, cellars, &c., will be let down and carefully fixed in position.

4.—Action During an Enemy Gas Attack.

(i) Should the gas cloud be unaccompanied by an infantry attack, the signal for gas will be sent and the S.O.S. signal will not be made unless an infantry attack developes.

Tactical Measures.

The troops in the front trenches will open a slow rate of rifle fire against the enemy trenches : occasional short bursts should be fired from machine guns to ascertain that these are in working order. All available howitzers should be turned on the enemy's trenches from which the gas is being emitted, or in which the enemy infantry may be concentrating for the assault.

(ii) Should an infantry attack develop, the normal procedure of S.O.S. will be carried out.

(iii) Troops in the front line must be prepared to bring a cross fire to bear on the enemy attempting to advance against a gassed portion of the line.

Movement.

(iv) **All movement must be reduced to a minimum. There should be as little moving about and talking as possible** in the trenches. Men must be made to realise that, with the gas now used by the enemy, the observance of this rule may be essential for their safety.

5.—Action After an Enemy Gas Attack.

Removal of Respirators, &c.

(i) Men in charge of anti-gas fans will use them as soon as the gas cloud has passed, so as to admit of respirators being removed.

(ii) Box respirators and helmets will not be removed after a gas attack until permission has been given by the Company Commander who will, when possible, ascertain from officers and N.C.Os. who have been trained at a Gas School that it is safe to do so.

Preparation for a Subsequent Attack.

(iii) So as to be ready for a subsequent gas cloud, all ranks will replace their box respirators or helmets in the " Alert " position.

A sharp look-out must be maintained for a repetition of the gas attack as long as the wind continues in the dangerous quarter.

Clearing of Shelters.

(iv) Dug-outs, cellars, &c., must not be entered before they have been thoroughly ventilated, except by men wearing box respirators or helmets. **Thorough ventilation, by means of fires or anti-gas fans, is the only sure way** of clearing a shelter.

Movement.

(v) No man suffering from the effects of gas is to be allowed to walk to the dressing station.

(vi) The clearing of trenches and dug-outs must not be carried out by men who have been affected by the gas.

(vii) After a gas attack, troops in the front trenches are to be relieved of all fatigue and carrying work for 24 hours by sending up working parties from companies in rear.

(viii) Horses which have been exposed to the gas should not be worked for 24 hours if it can be avoided.

Cleaning of Arms.

(ix) Rifles and machine guns must be cleaned after a gas attack. Oil cleaning will prevent corrosion for 12 hours, but the first opportunity must be taken to clean all parts in boiling water containing a little soda.

6.—Action During a Gas Shell Bombardment.

(i) Box respirators or helmets will be worn in the area shelled.

(ii) Arrangements must be made for giving a *local alarm* in the event of a sudden and intense bombardment with gas shells.

(iii) All dug-outs and shelters in the vicinity will be visited and any sleeping men roused.

APPENDIX V.

TYPICAL STANDING ORDERS FOR COMPANY GAS N.C.Os.

(i) They will assist officers at the inspection of box respirators, helmets and goggles and in making such local repairs as are possible. They will assist in training men in the use of anti-gas appliances.

(ii) Under the Company Commander they will have charge of all anti-gas trench stores as follows:—

(a) **Strombos Horns and Other Gas Alarm Devices.**—Inspect daily and see that sentries posted to them know how they should be used.

(b) **Gas-proof Shelters.**—See that the blanket doorways fit and are kept in good order.

(c) **Anti-gas Fans.**—See that they are in their proper position and in serviceable condition.

(d) **Stores of fuel** for clearing shelters.—Insure sufficient supply for clearing all dug-outs, to be maintained under company arrangements.

(e) **Vermorel Sprayers.**—Maintain in working order and see that supply of solution is available.

(f) **Gas Sampling Apparatus.**—Have charge of the vacuum bulbs and gas-testing tubes. Keep a stock of corked bottles and small tins with well-fitting lids for collecting samples of earth and water after a gas shell attack.

(iii) On relief they will assist the Company Commander in taking over all anti-gas trench stores. The Company Gas N.C.Os. should accompany the advance party and take over anti-gas trench stores (by daylight if possible).

(iv) They will make wind observations every three hours, or more frequently if the wind is in or nearing a dangerous quarter and will report any change of wind to the Company Commander.

(v) During a gas cloud attack they will take gas samples by means of the vacuum bulbs and gas-testing tubes.

(vi) During or after the attack the N.C.O. must note down in writing as much information regarding the attack as possible. (See Appendix VII.)

(vii) As soon as possible after the conclusion of a gas shell bombardment, the Gas N.C.O. must fill his bottles and tins (ii) (*f*) and take samples of water, mud, or earth from those parts of the line which are smelling most strongly of shell gases. He should note the position of any blind shells. (See Appendix VII.)

(viii) As soon as possible after a gas attack, all samples and notes will be handed in to the Company Commander for transmission to the Divisional Gas Officer.

APPENDIX VI.

INSTRUCTIONS FOR MAKING WIND OBSERVATIONS AND FURNISHING REPORTS.

Wind reports are to be made and handed to the Company Commander every three hours, or oftener if the wind is in or approaching a dangerous quarter. In order to make these reports the following points must be attended to :—

1.—Wind Vane.

A simple wind vane must be set up. *The vane must have as little friction as possible*, so that a wind of under 2 miles per hour will turn it. A little post at the top of the vane should carry a strip of linen 5 in. by $\frac{3}{4}$ in., by the movements of which the strength of the wind can be judged.

The vane must be set up sufficiently high to get a true observation (*e.g.*, 18 in. above the top of the dug-out, &c.). Correct orientation should be obtained by getting N by the N star and S by the sun at midday (Greenwich time).

2.—Direction of Wind.

Before reading the direction of the wind from the vane the observer should gauge the approximate direction by noting the course taken by smoke, &c. Direction of wind must be stated in points of the compass. The points of the compass to be used are shown in Fig. 8.

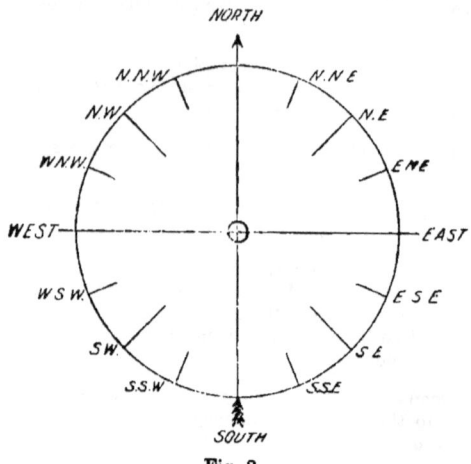

Fig. 8.

3.—Strength of Wind.

This may be judged from Beaufort's scale.

Beaufort's No.	Speed in m.p.h.	Observations of Natural objects.	Behaviour of flag at top of Vane.
0	0	Smoke straight up.	No movement.
1	2	Smoke slants.	No movement.
2	5	Felt on face.	Slight.
3	10	Paper, &c., moved.	$\frac{3}{4}$ up.
4	15	Bushes sway.	Up and falling often.
5	20	Tree tops sway. Wavelets on water.	Up. Falling less often.
6	30	Trees sway and whistle.	Up and flapping.

4.—Type of Report.

The points NORTH, SOUTH, EAST and WEST must be written in full. Other points are denoted by the usual letters.

The following example shows the type of report which should be made.

Wind Report.

Trench No. 131. Date 16.10.16.

Time.	Direction.	Speed.
6 p.m.	N.N.W.	12 m.p.h.

5.—Warning Available.

The following simple calculation determines the number of seconds which it will take for a gas cloud to move from the enemy's lines to our own:

Double trench distance (in yards) and divide by speed of wind (in m.p.h.). Example = $\frac{100 \times 2}{10} = 20$ seconds.

APPENDIX VII.

INSTRUCTIONS FOR TAKING GAS SAMPLES AND FOR REPORTING ON HOSTILE GAS ATTACKS.

1.—Taking Gas Samples during a Cloud Gas Attack.

A.—Vacuum Bulbs.

(*a*) Open the hinged lid at the end of the box containing the bulb.

(*b*) Remove the file from the plasticine stopping and with it make a scratch on the glass tube at the narrowest point.

(*c*) Hold the tube with finger and thumb of each hand and snap it where it is scratched; air will immediately rush in and fill the bulb.

(*d*) The box should be held as high as possible in the trench when the sample is taken.

(*e*) Press home the cap containing plasticine over the broken end of the tube so as to seal up the contents of the bulb.

Samples of gas should be taken both in the fire and support trenches. The first sample should be taken about *two* minutes after the commencement of the attack and other samples at intervals during the attack.

The exact time and place should be noted on the form on the back of the box immediately after the sample is taken.

If, when the gas waves have passed, any bulbs remain unused, samples of air in unprotected dug-outs should be taken before the latter are cleared.

Immediately after vacuum bulbs have been used they should be taken under shelter.

B.—Gas-Testing Tubes.

In the intervals of taking gas samples with vacuum bulbs a **Gas Testing Tube** should be used. Open the box by stripping off the adhesive plaster and pulling off the lid; pull out the small glass stopper and pump air through the apparatus by squeezing the rubber ball in the hand for 10 minutes. If the number of times the ball is squeezed is counted and recorded, useful information may be obtained. After the sample has been taken, replace the small glass stopper, and *at once* replace the lid of the box, taking care to avoid compressing the rubber ball. Note on the label the time and place at which the sample was taken.

2.—Collection of Specimens after a Gas Shell Bombardment.

As soon as possible after the conclusion of a gas shell bombardment, the Gas N.C.O. must take samples of water or earth from those parts of the line which are smelling most strongly of shell gases. He should note the spots at which the samples were taken.

During and after a gas attack the Gas N.C.O. should note down in writing as much information as possible on the following points :—

(a) Strength and direction of wind and general weather conditions.

(b) Times at which the gas wave or gas shell bombardment started and finished.

(c) Exact position and nature of place affected by gas or gas shells.

(d) Colour and colour changes of the gas cloud.

(e) Sound of escaping gas.

(f) Smell of gas and gas shells.

(g) Effect of gas and gas shells on men.

(h) To what extent telephone dug-outs, covered gun and machine gun emplacements, &c., were affected.

(i) The approximate number of gas shells used and their calibre.

(j) The position of blind shells and fragments of shells, &c.

3.—Forwarding of Samples, Specimens and Reports.

After an attack, cloud gas samples, gas testing tubes, gas shell bases and fragments, shell gas samples and notes on the attack will be handed to the Company Commander as soon as possible for transmission to the Divisional Gas Officer.

www.ingramcontent.com/pod-product-compliance
Lightning Source LLC
Chambersburg PA
CBHW070634050426
42450CB00011B/3197